IAN WHITCOMB'S
UKULELE
SING-ALONG

23 Classic and Fun Songs
with Uke Chords and Full Band Recordings

Ian Whitcomb

Alfred Music Publishing Co., Inc.
P.O. Box 10003
Van Nuys, CA 91410-0003
alfred.com

ISBN-10: 0-7390-7381-8 (Book & CD)
ISBN-13: 978-0-7390-7381-0 (Book & CD)

Cover Photos
Sailboat: © iStockphoto.com / o-che
Couple: © iStockphoto.com / Paul Kline

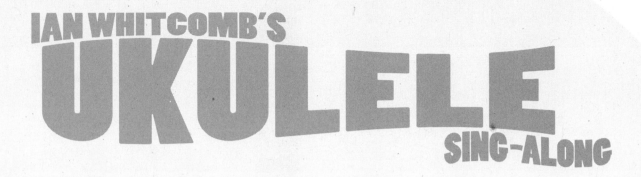

CONTENTS

March On to Happiness with Your Mighty Uke!

Who can resist our little four-stringed friend? The ukulele is the chosen weapon of mass delight: wherever ukesters are gathered together, bad guys scatter or collapse in mirth spasms, or, best of all, lay down their present arms to embrace the "Jumping Flea" and join our cheerful army. All over the world young and old are taking up the uke. From local societies meeting for humble monthly strumming and cocoa, to grand concerts where massed virtuoso orchestras enthrall with the high-speed picking of "The Flight of the Bumble Bee" or a bit of Wagner, the ukulele is taking its rightful place beside the once-almighty electric guitar.

This book is for all who simply want to have a good time either alone or with family, friends, and perhaps wider audiences later. The bulk of the songs here are sturdy standards from Tin Pan Alley, where music and words were written to be sung at mass gatherings in a show of togetherness. They're from a time when the community sing-along was a norm and the passivity of the couch potato age had not yet set in. Our selections range from the Hawaiian islands ("Aloha 'Oe" was written by a real Hawaiian queen) and the idyll of Dixie ("Waiting for the Robert E. Lee") through heartfelt hymns to life-giving Mother (an important figure who has been neglected by modern-day pop) and the healthful and slimming qualities of the Charleston (the daddy of all high-energy dances). You can woo the person of your choice with evergreen ballads like "Pretty Baby" and "You Made Me Love You (I Didn't Want to Do It)," then you can ease the tension with a comic number like "She Knows It." All these songs have verses that set up the story and the sentiment of the chorus.

I have included four of my own compositions that audiences at my shows enjoy singing along to. You can see this on YouTube if you search for "Have a Martini!" Other singers have taken to it too, as you'll see if you explore. Everyone seems to like singing "Martini" even if they're teetotalers. My wife Regina takes the lead on "Do I Love You? Yes I Do," a rather self-serving song that she delivers with a touchingly sweet passion. This too is on YouTube, as are many of the songs in the book.

I am joined on "Martini" and "Ambling Along" by Janet Klein, leader of The Parlor Boys, of which I'm a proud member. The recordings are from her CDs, and I'm grateful for her permission to use them.

It's really quite easy to produce a pleasing sound from the ukulele. I use the first finger with thumb support, like gripping a guitar pick, and then with a flick of the wrist I strum up and down. You can follow up the first finger flick with a fan of the three other fingers. This produces a roll effect and is impressive, but it needs to be used sparingly. The grids above the melody line show you where to place your fingers on the frets for the chords.

The harmonies haven't been simplified—Tin Pan Alley music was built on solid foursquare lines—but they're not hard to grasp. The beauty of only having four strings is that songs are stripped to their essentials, leaving no space for extra notes that, by extension, clog up the chords and result in a cocktail lounge pretentiousness. The chords are almost all in first position—at the top of your fretboard, near the tuning pegs. However, if you form a band, as I hope you will, then the slash lines under the chord symbols for guitar and keyboard (above the uke grid) will tell the bass and keyboard player what bass note to play and thus the correct inversion. You'll have a richer and more varied overall sound.

Sing and strum along to the recordings on the CD, and then proceed to perform in your own style.

All the songs on the CD are performed by me (vocals, ukulele, and accordion) accompanied by my Bungalow Boys. The tracks were recorded over the years in various locations, from the Hollywood Roosevelt Hotel's Blossom Room and the Alex Theatre in Glendale to studios both massive grand and garage humble.

WHERE DID ROBINSON CRUSOE GO WITH FRIDAY ON SATURDAY NIGHT?

Lyric by
SAM M. LEWIS
and JOE YOUNG

Music by
GEORGE W. MEYER

Where Did Robinson Crusoe Go With Friday on Saturday Night? - 2 - 1

Where Did Robinson Crusoe Go With Friday on Saturday Night? - 2 - 2

SHINE ON, HARVEST MOON

Words by
JACK NORWORTH

Music by
NORA BAYES – NORWORTH

Shine On, Harvest Moon - 2 - 1

I WANT A GIRL
(Just Like the Girl That Married Dear Old Dad)

Words by
WILLIAM DILLON

Music by
HARRY VON TILZER

Tempo di marcia

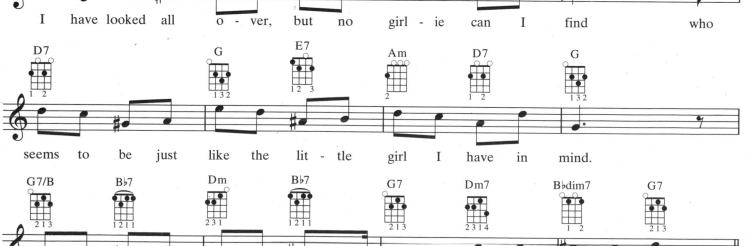

When I was a boy my moth - er of - ten said to me, "Get mar - ried boy and see how hap - py you will be." I have looked all o - ver, but no girl - ie can I find who seems to be just like the lit - tle girl I have in mind. I will have to look a - round un - til the right one I have found.

I Want a Girl - 2 - 1

M-O-T-H-E-R
(A Word That Means the World to Me)

Lyric by
HOWARD JOHNSON

Music by
THEODORE MORSE

Andante moderato

I've been a-round the world, you bet, but nev-er went to school. Hard knocks are all I seem to get, per-haps I've been a fool. But still, some ed-u-cat-ed folks, sup-posed to be so swell, would fail if they were called up-on a sim-ple word to spell. Now if you'd like to put me to the test,_____ there's one dear name that I can spell the best:

M-O-T-H-E-R - 2 - 1

13

M-O-T-H-E-R - 2 - 2

PRETTY BABY

Lyric by
GUS KAHN

Music by
TONY JACKSON and
EGBERT VAN ALSTYNE

BEAUTIFUL DREAMER

Words and Music by
STEPHEN FOSTER

Moderately

Beau - ti - ful dream - er, wake un - to me.

Star - light and dew - drops are wait - ing for thee.

Sounds of the rude world, heard in the day,

lulled by the moon - light have all passed a - way.

Beau - ti - ful dream - er, queen of my song,

Beautiful Dreamer - 2 - 1

list while I woo thee with soft mel - o - dy.

Gone are the cares of life's bus - y throng,

beau - ti - ful dream - er, a - wake un - to me!

beau - ti - ful dream - er, a - wake un - to me!

Verse 2:
Beautiful dreamer, out on the sea
Mermaids are chanting the wild lorelie;
Over the streamlet vapors are borne,
Waiting to fade at the bright coming moon.
Beautiful dreamer, beam on my heart,
E'en as the moon on the streamlet and sea
Then will all clouds of sorrow depart.
Beautiful dreamer, awake unto me!
Beautiful dreamer, awake unto me!

YAAKA HULA HICKEY DULA
(Hawaiian Love Song)

Words and Music by
E. RAY GOETZ, JOE YOUNG
and PETE WENDLING

Yaaka Hula Hickey Dula - 3 - 1

Have fun singing and playing along with the instrumental version on the recording.

ALOHA 'OE

Words and Music by
Queen Lili'uokalani

Verse 3:
Thus sweet memories come back to me
Bringing fresh remembrances of the past
Dearest one, yes, thou art mine own,
From thee true love shall ne'er depart.

I USED TO LOVE YOU BUT
IT'S ALL OVER NOW

Lyrics by
LEW BROWN

Music by
ALBERT VON TILZER

Marcia moderato

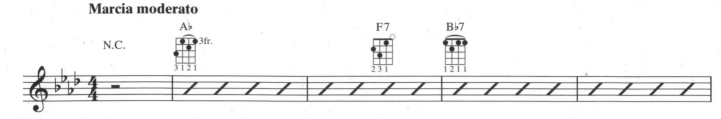

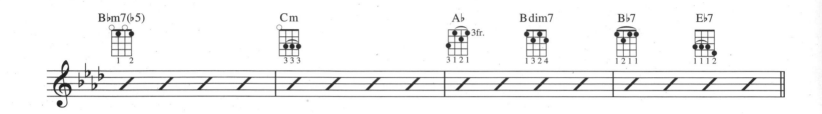

I used to bless the day I first met you.__ I planned so man-y things for

just us two.__ But now it's plain to see_____ that you have

nev - er cared for me. You can't de - ny you fooled me

from the start.__ It's best we part__ be-fore you break my heart.__

I Used to Love You but It's All Over Now - 2 - 1

I Used to Love You but It's All Over Now - 2 - 2

IF YOU WERE THE ONLY GIRL IN THE WORLD

Lyric by
CLIFFORD GREY

Music by
NAT D. AYER

Some - times_____ when I feel bad and things look blue,

I wish_____ a girl I had, say, one like you.

If You Were the Only Girl in the World - 2 - 1

WAITING FOR THE ROBERT E. LEE

Lyric by
L. WOLFE GILBERT

Music by
LEWIS F. MUIR

Waiting for the Robert E. Lee - 2 - 1

YOU MADE ME LOVE YOU
(I Didn't Want to Do It)

Lyric by
JOSEPH McCARTHY

Music by
JAMES V. MONACO

You made me want you. And all the time you knew it, I guess you al - ways knew it.

You made me hap - py some - times, you made me glad.

But there were times, dear, you made me feel__ so bad.____

You made me sigh for I did - n't want to tell you, I did - n't want to tell you,

I want some love that's true, yes I do, deed I do, you know I do.

Give me, give me, give me, give me what I cry__ for. You know you got the brand of kiss - es

that I'd die____ for. You know you made me love

1. you._____

2. you._____

SHE KNOWS IT

Words and Music by
JACK STERN and
CLARENCE J. MARKS

She Knows It - 3 - 1

32

knock-in' 'em cold___ and she knows it._____ She knows it._____ And beau-ty
knock-in' 'em cold___ and she knows it._____ She knows it._____ And she can

priz - es she's won___ in ev-'ry land 'neath the sun___ and she knows it,___ and___ she
dance, well I hope___ she floats like I - vo - ry soap___ and she knows it,___ and___ she

shows it._____ Ev-'ry-one in town tells me that she's a flirt____ and
shows it._____ She met the Prince of Wales here and his heart went, Bing!___ He

says that she's con-ceit-ed, but that does-n't hurt.____ She
said, "Be mine and you can have most an-y-thing."___ She

I don't give a dog-gone, she can have my shirt____ and she
said, "Come back and see me, Prince, when you're the King."___ And she

knows it,_____ and so do I. She's got a I.
knows it,_____ and so do

She Knows It - 3 - 3

DO I LOVE YOU? YES I DO!

Words and Music by
IAN WHITCOMB

Sweetly

Do I love you? Yes! I do!_____ And when you're out of my arms___ am I blue? Do you love me just as much as I love you?_____ Hope that this lit-tle song of love can make my dreams come true.

MANDY

Words and Music by
IRVING BERLIN

THE SHEIK OF ARABY

Lyric by
HARRY B. SMITH and
FRANCIS WHEELER

Music by
TED SNYDER

Moderato

Solo violin:

O - ver the des - ert wild and free_____

rides the bold Sheik of Ar - a - by._____

His Ar - ab band, at his com - mand,

fol - low his love's car - a - van._____

Un - der the shad - ow of the palms_____

he sings to call her to his arms._____ "I'm the

The Sheik of Araby - 2 - 1

MARGIE

Lyric by
BENNY DAVIS

Music by
CON CONRAD and
J. RUSSEL ROBINSON

Moderato

You can talk a - bout your love af - fairs,_____

here's one I must tell to you._____

All night long they sit up - on the stairs._____

He holds her close and starts to coo,_____ "My lit - tle

Mar - gie,_____ I'm al - ways think - ing of you.

Margie - 2 - 1

CAROLINA IN THE MORNING

Lyric by
GUS KAHN

Music by
WALTER DONALDSON

Moderato

Wish-ing is good_ time wast-ed. Still, it's a hab-it, they say.

Wish-ing for sweets_ I've tast-ed, that's all I do___ all day.

May-be there's noth-ing in wish-ing, but speak-ing of wish-ing, I'll say:

Noth-ing could be fin-er than to be in Car-o-li-na in the morn-

ing. No one could be sweet-er than my sweet-ie when I meet her in the

morn-ing. Where the morn-ing

Carolina in the Morning - 2 - 1

Carolina in the Morning - 2 - 2

PEG O' MY HEART

Words by
ALFRED BRYAN

Music by
FRED FISCHER

Moderately

N.C.

1. Oh! My

heart's in a whirl___ o - ver one lit - tle girl.___ I love her, I love___ her, yes, I
2. *See additional lyrics*

do!___ Al - though her heart is far a - way,___ I hope to make her mine some -

day.___ Ev - 'ry beau - ti - ful rose,___ ev - 'ry vi - o - let knows___ I

love her, I love___ her fond and true,___ and her heart fond - ly sighs___ as I

sing to her eyes,___ her eyes of blue,___ sweet eyes of blue, my dar - ling!

Peg o' My Heart - 2 - 1

Peg o' my heart,_____ I love you. We'll nev - er part._____

_____ I love you, dear lit - tle girl,_____ sweet lit - tle girl,_____

sweet-er than the Rose of Er - in are your win - ning smiles en - dear - in'. Peg o' my heart,_____

_____ your glanc - es with I - rish art_____ en - trance us.

Come, be my own,_____ come, make your home_____ in my

heart.

Verse 2:
When your heart's full of fears
And your eyes full of tears,
I'll kiss them, I'll kiss them all away.
For, like the gold that's in your hair,
Is all the love for you I bear.
O, believe in me, do.
I'm as lonesome as you.
I miss you, I miss you all the day.
Let the light of love shine from your eyes into mine,
And shine for aye,
Sweetheart for aye, my darling!

AMBLING ALONG

Words and Music by
IAN WHITCOMB

Ambling Along - 4 - 1

People bus - tle 'round and 'round, hus - tling night and day.

We just look and laugh be - cause we go a dif - f'rent way...

Am - bling a - long in the sun - shine,

am - bling a - long in the rain,_____

we take our time as the world rush - es by,_____

we keep our eyes on the sea and the sky._____

46

Ambling Along - 4 - 3

Am - bling a - long with-out wor - ries, smil - ing 'cause we've

got no stocks or shares. We've no need for tel - e - phones,

all we hear are bird-ies' bell-tones: "Tweet-y-tweet, tweet-y-tweet, tweet-y-tweet tweet!"

Got no mon-ey! *(stamp foot)* Got no cares!

Patter, as first chorus of song is played by the band:
IAN: Hello, Janet!
JANET: Hello, Ian! How are you?
IAN: Oh, not so dusty.
JANET: Yes, I've been on the move, too.
IAN: Not that awful landlord again?
JANET. No, no—my new landlords are the sea and the sky.
IAN: Same here—it's the open road for me.
JANET: What have you been up to?
IAN: Oh, this and that.
JANET: And a little bit of the other?
IAN: Just a leetle bit!
JANET & IAN: JUST A LEETLE BIT!
JANET: You used to have plans to be a Big Man, a Head Man.
IAN: I did, I certainly did!
JANET: You said you'd become the King of Hi Tiddly Hi Ti Island.
IAN: Yes—and have all those oojahs and elling-phants.
JANET: What happened?
IAN: I didn't fancy the traveling—or the sleeping arrangements when I got there.
JANET: Well—now we're both in the same pickle. Salted and serene. Just ambling along.
IAN: Not racing madly to Nowhere Land.
JANET: Exactly! We're the King and Queen of Relaxavoo!
IAN: I didn't know you spoke French.
JANET: Just a leetle bit.
(Into verse of song followed by Chorus:)

HAVE A MARTINI!

Words and Music by
OLIVER DE COLOGNE
(aka IAN WHITCOMB)

Have a Martini! - 2 - 1

GOODNIGHT

Words and Music by
IAN WHITCOMB

Medium beat

Good - night to you___ and see___ ___ you once a - gain. I hope___ that you___ ___ will miss___ me now and then. I know___ ___ the glow___ of your___ ap - plause will burn, but I hope that you got some - thing in___ re - turn. ___ Good - night___ to you,___

Goodnight - 2 - 1

Have fun singing and playing along with the instrumental version on the recording.

CHARLESTON

Words and Music by
CECIL MACK and
JIMMY JOHNSON

Charleston - 3 - 1

Discography

1988 *Happy Days Are Here Again* (Audiophile ACD 242)

1992 *Ian Whitcomb's Ragtime America* (ITW 009)

1994 *We're Talking Ragtime* (Stomp Off CD 1276)

1995 *Lotusland—A New Kind of Old-Fashioned Musical Comedy* (Audiophile ACD 283)

1996 *Let the Rest of the World Go By* (Audiophile ACD 267)

1997 *The Golden Age of Lounge* (Varese Sarabande VSD 5821)

1997 *Ian Whitcomb: You Turn Me On!/Mod Mod Music Hall* (Sundazed SC 11044)

1997 *Titanic: Music as Heard on the Fateful Voyage* (Rhino R2 72821)

1998 *Spread a Little Happiness* (Audiophile ACD 249)

1998 *Titanic Tunes—A Sing-A-Long in Steerage* (The Musical Murrays conducted by Ian Whitcomb) (Varese Sarabande 5965)

1998 *Songs from the Titanic Era* (The New White Star Orchestra) (Varese Sarabande VSF 5966)

1998 *You Turn Me On—The Very Best of Ian Whitcomb* (Varese Sarabande VSD 5897)

1999 *Comedy Songs* (Audiophile ACD 163)

2001 *Sentimentally Yours* (Woodpecker Records)

2002 *Dance Hall Days* (ITW Records)

2003 *Under the Ragtime Moon* (Vivid Sound B00008WD18)

2003 *Pianomelt* (Muskrat RATCD 004)

2003 *Ian Whitcomb in Hollywood* (Muskrat RATCD 005)

2003 *Ian Whitcomb's Red Hot Blue Heaven* (Muskrat RATCD 002)

2003 *Crooner Tunes* (Muskrat RATCD 003)

2005 *Old Chestnuts & Rare Treats* (ITW Records)

2005 *Words & Music* (ITW Records)

2006 *Lone Pine Blues* (Vivid Sound NACD3229; Japanese import only)

2008 *Ready for You* (Janet Klein and her Parlor Boys) (Coeur De Jeannette)

2010 *Whoopee Hey! Hey!* (Janet Klein and her Parlor Boys) (Coeur De Jeannette)

All tracks on the enclosed CD were performed between 1965 and 2010 by Ian Whitcomb on vocals, accompanied by his orchestras, dance bands, and Bungalow Boys, except:

Tracks 2 & 8: Janet Klein & Ian Whitcomb with The Parlor Boys

Track 6: vocals by Ian & Regina Whitcomb

Tracks 17 & 23: piano by Professor Richard Zimmerman

Track 1: Hawaiian slide guitar by Fred Sokolow

All ukulele, banjolele, and piano accordion by Ian Whitcomb.

All tracks licensed from ITW Records.

About the Author

Ian Whitcomb, born in England in 1941, has been performing pop songs since childhood. He grew up on classic music hall and the hits of the day. At boarding school in the 1950s, he introduced his version of rock 'n' roll, leading his boy band on three-chord guitar. In his late teens, he discovered ragtime and rhythm & blues. He also discovered a discarded ukulele at his cousin's house and took to it mightily.

While studying history at Trinity College Dublin in the early 1960s, he recorded a song he'd made up for Bluesville, his blues group. "You Turn Me On" shot him into the American top 10 in 1965. As a crazy piano-pounding rock star, Whitcomb toured with The Rolling Stones and The Beach Boys. But his interest in the roots of pop, especially ragtime and Tin Pan Alley (in 1966 he scored a minor hit with his ukulele-based version of 1916's "Where Did Robinson Crusoe Go with Friday on Saturday Night?"), caused him to neglect his teen idol career in order to concentrate on researching and performing this music.

The result has been a flow of books, records, documentaries, radio shows, and concerts celebrating the pop of the pre-rock era. Ian's first book, *After the Ball: Pop Music from Rag to Rock*, published in 1972, is now an acknowledged classic. He's appeared at the Hollywood Bowl, the Montreux Jazz Festival, and with Johnny Carson on *The Tonight Show*—always spreading the word. He has presented a radio show since 1980, starting at KROQ and moving to NPR affiliates KCRW and KPCC. Recently, he's taken his show to the Internet at XM/Sirius satellite radio.

In 1998 he produced the CD *Titanic: Music as Heard on the Fateful Voyage,* which won a Grammy. He managed to slip in a little ukulele.

He provided songs and performance for the movie *Stanley's Gig,* the story of an obsessive uke player. Ian's uke-based music can be heard in over a dozen other movies, including *The Cat's Meow* and *Last Call*. All this work significantly contributed to inspiring the current revival of the ukulele.

Ian's musical adventures and misadventures in and around his house in Altadena, California—which he shares with his singing and cooking wife Regina (not forgetting "Ukie," the old Martin)—can be enjoyed in his latest book, *Letters from Lotusland: An Englishman in Exile,* obtainable everywhere, but especially from his website at ianwhitcomb.com.